CH00400498

Introduction by Lady Broers

In these pages you will find 50 portraits of outstanding Cambridge alumnae. These women make a very significant contribution to the country, and the world, in medicine, law, government, religion, education, science, journalism and the arts.

Ever since the first pioneering women students began to study in Cambridge in the late 1860s, Cambridge has produced exceptional alumnae. The women photographed here represent all surviving generations, spanning from those who were at Cambridge in the 1910s to current students. They represent a broad range of professions and important public roles, and most of the University's thirty-one Colleges. Although they come from very different backgrounds, all of the portrait subjects have shown the determination to make their hard-won Cambridge education count.

These portraits, by the highly regarded photographer, Julia Hedgecoe, comprised an exhibition to mark the fiftieth anniversary of the first admission of women to Cambridge degrees. I hope that they will inspire the next generations of Cambridge alumnae, and encourage women of all backgrounds to consider applying for their own place at Cambridge.

Mary J. Broers.

Lady Broers has led the *Educating Eve* project since its conception. She has lived in Cambridge since 1984; her husband, Prof. Sir Alec Broers, is the current Vice-Chancellor of the University of Cambridge.

Diane Abbott MP

Newnham College, 1973
History
MP for Hackney North and Stoke Newington

I am glad that I attended Cambridge University. It is a fine institution. I learned a lot about history and even more about myself and my personal values. Being a Cambridge graduate from a working class background has informed my politics and philosophy of life.

Jobeda Ali

Trinity College, 1993
English and History
Head of the Group to Encourage Ethnic Minority Applications

What surprised me most about the students at Cambridge University was that they did not reflect the values and interests of the 'upper/middle classes' as I expected. More than anything, they reflected concerns and activities current amongst students nationally. At Cambridge today, attitudes towards career and travel ambitions, government politics, sex, drugs, sexuality, race, religion, health, gender and the stance towards animal and human rights are a reflection of our generation, not our social background – a concept which to this generation is too ambiguous to be meaningful.

Dame Margaret Anstee DCMG

Newnham College, 1944
Modern and Medieval Languages
First woman to head a United Nations peace keeping mission (Angola)
Adviser to the President and Government of Bolivia

*Newnham opened a magic door for me onto a world I had hardly dared to
contemplate. As an only child born into a working-class rural family I had
spent wartime schooldays secluded in an Essex village, following a relentless
regime of study in order to win the scholarships that provided the only way
to finance my education. Books and examinations of course continued to
loom large at Cambridge, but I also discovered a new and exciting life of
culture, art, theatre and lively debate on every subject under the sun, as well
as more frivolous social activities hitherto unknown to me. This heady
combination was not only intellectually stimulating but also played a key
part in developing my personality and self-confidence.*

The Hon Mrs Justice Arden DBE

Girton College, 1968
Law
High Court Judge and Chairman of the Law Commission

If I close my eyes, and think about my University days, I see colleges, staircases, the long, anonymous corridors of Girton and people moving with remarkable speed, as if my memory was on fast forward. Cambridge was and is a place for lively individuals with creative minds, and also for making lasting friendships. There, amid the endless mugs of coffee, the countless bikes, the constant chatter and debate and the all-pervasive busyness of everyone, I discovered that the world is full of challenges to be overcome. Cambridge gave me the confidence that even I might be able to make some contribution.

Professor Dame Gillian Beer FBA

Girton College, 1965
English
President of Clare Hall; Chair of The Booker Prize Committee 1997

Cambridge has shaped and extended my adult life in a number of diverse ways: as a scholar, with the wonderful resources of the University Library; as a teacher, in the opportunity to work with gifted people from such a variety of backgrounds; as a parent, at the school gates where I have met so many lasting friends; and as an intellectual worker, through talk with colleagues in different disciplines. Girton gave me a start as a Research Fellow and sustained me for much of my career; Clare Hall allows me now to explore the international dimension of Cambridge life with its exuberant mix of graduates, university officers, and visiting fellows from all parts of the world.

Professor Jocelyn Bell Burnell FRAS FInstP

New Hall, 1965
Physics
First woman physics professor in the UK, at the Open University

I'm sure the graduate student experience of Cambridge differs from the undergraduate experience, but nonetheless those three years as a research student changed my life.

Dr Anna Bidder

Newnham College, 1926
Natural Sciences and Zoology
Co-founder of Lucy Cavendish College

Cambridge-born, of a zoologist father and a physiologist mother, myself a zoologist, academia has been the background of my life, colouring all my thinking. Among many treasures, I learnt to value highly integrity of thought and feeling, and the stimulus of discussion of all kinds and at all depths, and to welcome 'We do not know' as a source of impetus to re-thinking and re-search. In middle age, I identified a horrible intellectual snobbery, which I can discipline but cannot hope to eradicate.

Dame Ann Bowtell DCB

Girton College, 1957
Economics
Permanent Secretary, Department of Social Security

*Cambridge simply changed my life. My generation was the first in my
family to go to University, let alone Cambridge. The beauty, the libraries,
the peace, the company, the exhaustion of working hard and playing hard,
the self-confidence of finding you could succeed academically and socially in
a place like this. The images are still with me: the soothing peace of Girton
library, the gloom of those long corridors at winter tea times, the cold cycle
rides back at night. Cambridge set me out on my future career, and there I
met my future husband.*

Dr Margaret Bray

Churchill College, 1972
Mathematics and Economics
Reader at the London School of Economics

I came to Cambridge in 1972 as one of the first women undergraduates at Churchill College. I read Mathematics for Part I and Economics for Part II. Coming from a family of sisters, and a girls' school, I learnt at Cambridge to live as one of a small minority of women. This was an important lesson, because I went on to be an academic economist, a profession where women are still very much in the minority. Undergraduate life was sometimes fascinating, often fun, at times hard going. But nothing was as hard as marking a huge pile of examination scripts as a very pregnant lecturer.

Victoria Brignell

Downing College, 1994
Classics
Winner of a Varsity Trust Bursary for a course in newspaper journalism

*I have many fond memories of Cambridge and I made some great friends
there. The work was tough (and I can't say I miss the exams!) but we also
managed to enjoy a rollercoaster social life – numerous trips to films and
plays, chaotic pancake parties, exuberant Christmas formal halls, subversive
revues and surreal midnight walks along the Fen Causeway come to mind.
Highlights included meeting my hero Barbara Castle, dining with Inspector
Morse's creator and becoming CUSU's [Cambridge University Students
Union] Students with Disabilities Officer.*

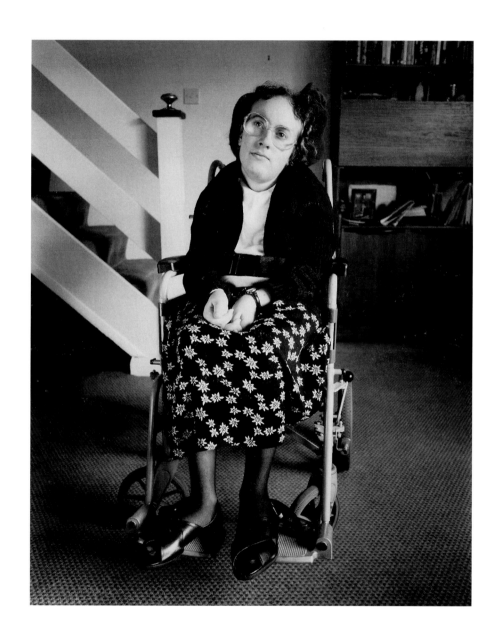

The Baroness Brigstocke

Girton College, 1947
Classics
Former head of St Paul's Girls' School

Trite though it may sound, Cambridge changed my life, opening up opportunities that I had never dreamed of during my wartime school days. I found I could act: my first visit abroad after the war was to Sweden with the ADC as Mrs Clandon in You Never Can Tell – *the title itself an augury for my future.*

Eleanor Bron

Newnham College, 1957
Modern and Medieval languages
Actress and Writer

My headmistress persuaded me to try for university instead of drama school. I ended up being an actress anyway. Quite a few do these days – and perhaps by now the equation actress = dimwit is no longer automatic. Cambridge introduced me to people and ways of thinking I might never have encountered and still value. For me, three years of unattached exploration and discovery were a crucial luxury – what I once described as being "... – at a particularly open moment in our lives, momentarily poised like passengers in an unusually well appointed transit lounge...". I look back at an enlightened era and my gratitude goes on.

Dr Alison Brown

Sidney Sussex College, 1976
Engineering
President of NAVSYS and Global Positioning System expert

The only bad part about being in the first year of women at Sidney Sussex was not having the critical mass yet for a college eight. The vivid pace of life at college was exhilarating. I remember my tutor counselling not just to spend time on studying, but also to savour the other pursuits offered by Cambridge. Despite the effect on my first two tripos exams, the experience (and fun) that I gained from taking this recommendation to heart has been of much value in my career. Cambridge to me always conveys a sense of timelessness, I am honoured to be part of its history.

Jess Brown

Girton College, 1922
Natural Sciences
Teacher

*I went to Girton in October 1922, to read Natural Science and presented
myself for the Tripos in Chemistry, Botany, Zoology and Physiology in June
1925 and received my Titular Degree. I felt extremely privileged and loved
every day – the work which was a revelation to me, the games, so
competitive and satisfying (hockey blue) and above all, the company. The
effect on my later life was enormous. My husband (Queens' 1921-24) was
lost with* HMS Abdiel *in 1943. So in 1944 I returned to teaching
professionally and was able to give our three children the best of all gifts – a
sound education.*

The Revd Georgina Byrne

Corpus Christi College, 1996
Theology
Assistant Chaplain, Corpus Christi College

I spent three years living in Cambridge. For two of those years I was training for ordained ministry at Westcott House, in the third year I completed an MPhil in Church History at Corpus Christi College, and was there simultaneously a post-graduate student and an honorary assistant chaplain. Having now left Cambridge, I am aware that my memories are largely dominated by all things ecclesiastical. In spite of (or possibly because of?) this, the memories are also filled with many amazing and inspiring people: those long dead, whom I studied in the UL [University Library], and those very much alive, with whom I lived.

Left to right: The Revds Dr Jo Bailey Wells, Georgina Byrne and Dr Emma Hebblethwaite

The Revd Dr Emma Hebblethwaite

Corpus Christi College, 1984
Theology
Chaplain, King's College

Having spent most of my time in Cambridge since matriculation, apart from a couple of years as a curate in Suffolk, I feel Cambridge has been a vital part of my life. And when I think of Cambridge, I think especially of the people I have known and loved here. That's how Cambridge educates one – through the people one encounters; the memories of those I have known still speak to me from the past and I know that there are others I am yet to meet. This place – through its people – has quite simply made me what I am, and I have been blessed in the people I have known at my three Colleges: Corpus, Westcott, and King's.

The Revd Dr Jo Bailey Wells

Corpus Christi College, 1984
Natural Sciences
Chaplain, Clare College

It was during my second year as an undergraduate, over a meal, that a friend first suggested I might consider ordination. I threw my bread roll at him in disgust. But I realise that three years at Corpus probably did more to form me and enable me than any other period of my life so far. I was immersed in a stimulating community of scholarship – and of sport, and of spirituality – that refused to leave me comfortable. I continue to treasure those influential friendships, whilst I now work to build the same kind of honest, engaging community in Clare College.

Anne Campbell MP FISS FIS FRSA

Newnham College, 1959
Mathematics
MP for Cambridge

Cambridge in 1959 gave me a completely different view of the world from the one I had known. It allowed me to think, to be my own person and to feel very proud that I was continuing the august tradition that had been established by so many women before me.

The Rt Hon Baroness David

Newnham College, 1932
English
Politician and education campaigner

Coming to Cambridge in 1932 fulfilled a long-standing ambition. I was not disappointed. It was thrilling to be here, and I had never enjoyed so much freedom. There were rules, but they did not seem too onerous at the time, and were occasionally broken. There were stimulating people to meet, work was fun. The friends I made here remained friends for the rest of my life; we could easily pick up where we left off. And I met my husband here.

Margaret Drabble CBE

Newnham College, 1957
English Literature
Author

My days at Newnham were very happy. Both my parents had been to Cambridge, and had given me great expectations. These were more than fulfilled. I enjoyed the work, I made good friends, and I was very fortunate to be active in the theatre there at a time when some very fine actors and directors were discovering their gifts. My adult life began at Cambridge. After some years in a traditional girls' boarding school, the sense of freedom was exhilarating, and the intellectual companionship has lasted through my life. I enjoyed it all. I even enjoyed sitting my examinations.

Alison Duke

Girton College, 1934
Classics
One of the longest-serving academics at Girton College

As for my feelings (about the University of Cambridge) in the late 1930s, we were not so deprived as some of the earlier generations – but I did resent the rather scruffy 'titular' degree statement, and the absence of an actual graduation – a disappointing end, if one had worked hard for a good degree. But I was very grateful that the University elected me to a Graduate Scholarship – these awards were nearly all open to women by my time.

Haruko Fukuda

New Hall, 1965
History
Member of the governing council of The Nikko Research Center

My three years at Cambridge inspired an interest in many of the areas of life which have given me so much fulfilment – History, Art, Literature, Architecture, Society, and Disputation: a sound sextet for a career in commerce, as I soon found when I began to be invited to City lunches. Those years left me with a lasting respect for scholars and for scholarship. I remember with particular gratitude Dame Rosemary Murray, the Founder of New Hall and President of the College throughout my time, the late Dr Helen Clover, my Director of Studies in History, and my Tutor, Dr Hope Hammond with whom I have kept in close contact ever since.

Dr Jane Goodall CBE

Newnham College, 1961
Zoology
Primatologist and Conservationist

After several years studying chimpanzees at Gombe in Tanzania, working at Cambridge for my PhD taught me scientific self-discipline and to couch my findings in scientific terms. Having a PhD from Cambridge helped open many doors for me in the early years.

Paula Gould

Queens' College, 1991
Natural Sciences, History and Philosophy of Science
PhD student and winner of two national writing competitions in 1997

When I arrived in Cambridge as an undergraduate in October 1991, I had absolutely no idea that I would still be here in 1998.

Gunn Chit Wha LLB

Girton College, 1948
Law
Lawyer practicing in Malaysia

*After four difficult years under the Japanese Military Occupation in the then
known Malay Peninsula, I was happy and excited to leave for England for
further education. Girton was chosen as my father was at Peterhouse and
he was ambitious for his children to go up to Cambridge. Despite the
complete change of lifestyle my undergraduate days were happy and
memorable. Good friends helped me to overcome homesickness. Friendships
made with people from different countries and cultural backgrounds
instilled in me a wider perspective of the world and in the aims and
activities of the United Nations Association in the University. The changing
of the Seasons was exciting to one who grew up in the Tropics, but I had to
bear the cold damp weather as Girton had no central heating and we had to
survive with only three scuttles of coal (full of slate) per week. Surprisingly,
life in such an environment with post-war food rationing and thrice daily
cycling to and from town kept me in excellent health. I remember with
affection and gratitude my Law Tutors for their excellent supervisions and
guidance at all times, which helped me through my Law examinations and
equipped me for my legal career.*

Jane Heal FBA

New Hall, 1964
History and Moral Sciences
Reader in Philosophy at St John's College, Cambridge

Four institutions have provided the framework for the times when I have lived and worked in Cambridge – three colleges (New Hall, Newnham and St John's) and the Faculty of Philosophy. Each of them, in its own particular way, means to me what Cambridge means to me, namely a distinctive combination of respect for individuality with collegiality. In Cambridge one can pursue one's own intellectual projects, but in the context of a community of friends and colleagues who enjoy the exchange of ideas. For a certain kind of academic temperament, what more could one ask?

Phyllis Hetzel

Newnham College, 1937
History
Former President of Lucy Cavendish College, Registrar of the Roll at
Newnham College

*In 1937, Newnham College awarded me a major scholarship, without
which my hope of university education was a pipe dream. With it I entered
a new world, where to read and think was honoured; and where it was
right to make discoveries in art and architecture, music and acting, travel,
and rambling and fencing. What a contrast to the limits of my impoverished
home life. To Newnham and Cambridge I owe a successful profession, and
an enriched life. I hope my successors enjoy similar benefits.*

HE Judge Rosalyn Higgins DBE QC

Girton College, 1955
Law
First woman judge at the International Court of Justice

Cambridge is magic. This is so commonly said. But to a grammar school student, coming from a family where no one had been to university at all, Cambridge was indeed true magic. It was to pass through a door into an extraordinarily intense world, physically beautiful and intellectually exciting. It was a world where anything was now possible – and indeed it turned out to be.

Dorothea Hutchinson

Newnham College, 1926
English
Psychiatric social worker

When I came to Newnham College I had already spent the whole of my life in Cambridge as I was born and bred in a highly academic family. My father was a professor and my two older brothers both did well at their colleges, one of them really brilliantly. This set a high standard for me to emulate but, unfortunately, I was very shy and lacking in confidence. Life at Newnham helped considerably and I made some really close and lasting friendships. The college fellows were helpful too, especially Miss Dale who was tutor of Old Hall where I lived, and Miss Welsford who encouraged my interest in English Literature. Miss Dale sensed that several of us were worried as to what we should do when we left Newnham and she arranged for a speaker to come and tell us about social work and that completely solved it for me.

Lady Jeffreys (Bertha Swirles)

Girton College, 1921
Mathematics
Mathematician

In 1921 I came to Girton from Northampton School for Girls where I had been taught by three Cambridge women mathematicians. I am proud to have belonged as a scholar, and for sixty years as a Fellow, to pioneer the College founded in 1869 by Emily Davies and others. At Cambridge and at other Universities, I have played a part in educating both Adam and Eve. Cambridge has meant for me a marriage of nearly fifty years and many lasting friendships.

Sarah Jones

St John's College, 1987
Modern and Medieval Languages
President of Wintercomfort for the Homeless and Education Officer at
Cambridge Arts Cinema

*I arrived at St John's in Autumn 1987 not knowing what to expect but very
much looking forward to what I knew would be four years of excitement
and terror combined. I remember being struck by how much easier it was to
find people I could get on with – I had imagined that most people would
hail from backgrounds far more impressive than my own, and although they
probably did, most of the time this was not apparent.*

*I left Cambridge in '91 knowing that a City career was not for me but not
too sure about the alternatives. I'm glad I eventually found other things to
do, but equally delighted to now find myself back in Cambridge and
collaborating with Fellows at St John's, both through work at
Wintercomfort for the Homeless and at the Arts Cinema, both 'city'
organisations. Undoubtedly, it is this interaction between community and
university which is crucial if Cambridge is to exploit its full potential and
become a more satisfying city for all its inhabitants, inside and out of the
university.*

Dr Olga Kennard OBE FRS

Newnham College, 1942
Natural Sciences
Director of Research, Cambridge Crystallographic Data Centre

I came up to Cambridge in 1942, just three years after leaving Hungary. Three war years filled with school work and struggle to adapt to a new country. Cambridge was a revelation and an inspiration: new subjects, fun in working, friendships, and involvement in a multitude of earnest and not so earnest University societies. Cambridge set me on the path of a scientific career in crystallography and the foundation and development of a world-renowned centre for scientific information. I can not imagine what my life would have been had I not passed the hurdle of the Newnham entrance.

Denise Kingsmill

Girton College, 1965
Archaeology and Anthropology
Deputy Chairman, Monopolies and Mergers Commission

As I walked for the first time down the Girton drive, between the huge horse chestnut trees, I had a powerful sense of being in the right place, of belonging. 'My life starts here', I thought. For the next three years Girton was, for me, the calm rational place I returned to at the end of each day spent coping with the hurly-burly of Cambridge life in the Sixties where we were, as women undergraduates, still a minority group. Girton gave me comfort, courage and confidence to succeed in other male-dominated worlds where I have spent my career.

Dr Penelope Leach

Newnham College, 1959
History
Psychologist and childcare expert

Getting into Cambridge filled me with astonishment; a minor scholarship to Newnham frothed it up like champagne bubbles. Three miserable years at a pretentious fourth rate boarding school had left me feeling totally stupid and although the Perse School (to which I was released for A levels) told me I was 'Cambridge material' I did not really believe it. I am still thankful for the privilege of three years in the most beautiful University town in the world filled with fascinating words from the past (I did read a lot though more psychology than history) and witty ones in the present (we thought we were funny, anyway). With fees covered by State grants, residential colleges as places of safety and a tutorial system for all, Cambridge offered a protected personal freedom that's almost unknown to today's University students. I did a little work, a lot of acting and an enormous amount of growing up. It qualified me for nothing except becoming a grown-up and getting qualifications.

Cambridge was part of my own past and future too. My mother, Elisabeth Walsh, was at Newnham (far more an accomplishment then, of course); so was my older sister, Prue (my younger sister, Freja, was at New Hall) and so eventually was my daughter Melissa Leach. Three generations of feminists at women's colleges. Will Cambridge still be Mecca for a fourth?

Rosalyn Liu

Trinity College, 1996
Law
President of the Association of British and Chinese University Students

I arrived in Cambridge with limited experience, but in my two years here I have been President of a university society, participated in the first ever Model United Nations to be held in Spain, risen at insanely early hours to cox eight other equally tired but determined students, studied at the Goethe Institute in Bavaria within sight of the German-Austrian Alps, and helped to hold the Trinity College May Ball 1998 for over 2000 people. In between, I have been known to attempt the study of Law.

Professor Joanna MacGregor

New Hall, 1978
Music
Pianist and Honorary Fellow of the Royal Academy of Music

Cambridge was initially a difficult experience – overwhelming and full of freshers who already knew each other. When I found my feet I especially enjoyed Hugh Wood's inspired eclectic teaching. Cambridge gave me the chance to find out what I didn't like, as well as what I did – passions that have stayed with me, and an insatiable curiosity.

Molly Maxwell

Newnham College, 1914
English and German
Oldest graduate of Cambridge University at 104

I went up to Newnham in 1914 to read English and German. I enjoyed my three years there very much – especially since I came from a remote country village. Of course, life was a little restricted because we were not allowed to mix very freely with the few men who were not in the forces. We could chat with a male acquaintance if we met in the street but could not visit his rooms or go to tea alone. Nevertheless we found plenty of activities: I especially enjoyed rowing and I remember we once rowed as far as Ely (and back!) – a crew of four girls and a cox. The most notable lecturer was Sir Arthur Quiller-Couch, who, however, took very little notice of the largely female audience, and addressed all his remarks to the one or two males, as 'Men of the World'.

I know that the Cambridge experience has enriched the whole of my life.

Rabbi Julia Neuberger

Newnham College, 1969
Oriental Studies
Britain's first woman rabbi

Not the best time of my life, but wonderful nevertheless. A basis for learning how to think, to act, to make a difference – in a very small way. The place I learned to cook, and to drink, and to write articles. But my fondest memory is of the academic work. Though I did not become an academic myself, the love of the subject, the love of books, the sheer atmosphere of scholarship, was a great delight.

Sarah Nichols

New Hall, 1982
English and Social and Political Science
Marketing and Information Services Manager, Cambridge University Press

Cambridge stretched me intellectually, made me question my surroundings and gave me confidence. (New Hall was, I think, particularly good at nurturing the diffident female student.) Just as educational was living the student life and the long-term entrenchment of some bad habits. All of these things have stood me in good stead.

Frances Partridge FRSL

Newnham College, 1918
English and Moral Sciences
Author, last surviving member of the Bloomsbury Group

What more perfect setting for the euphoria of youth could there be than Cambridge with its idyllic beauty, surprising inhabitants, and a mental climate in which ideas sprouted, grew and changed shape?

Penny Pereira

King's College, 1995
English
Cambridge University Students' Union Women's Officer

After three years I'm no longer so drawn by the charming arrogance of Cambridge, although I've greatly valued the opportunities and perspectives it has provided me. As Women's Officer this year I've been deeply inspired by the strong movement of men and women determined to challenge those inequalities that remain within the institution.

Rachel Quarmby

Fitzwilliam College, 1989
English
Administrator for the English National Opera

Cambridge gave me the most extraordinary opportunities to participate in activities both thrilling and terrifying that would never have presented themselves to me except within the charmed world of its domain. The faith of my peers that I could: produce an opera, row in an eight, was both touching and empowering. Cambridge's other enduring legacy to me is that it was the place that witnessed the passionate start of lifelong friendships, and nurtured their growth into maturity.

Kathleen Raine FRSL

Girton College, 1926
Natural Sciences and Material Sciences
Winner of the Queen's Gold Medal for Poetry and biographer of Blake
and Yeats

*My life in College seemed at first like a dream, a painted scene, as if life
here were made of a different stuff from any reality I had hitherto known;
as in a sense it was, thought not in the way I thought. The difference lay in
no magic light cast on the scene, but in a kind of consciousness; in what, for
educated people constitutes reality; to what themes, experiences,
happenings, the attention of the mind is directed; what is noted, what
disregarded. I did not see what were the demands made upon those who,
like myself, wished to participate. I thought, paddler that I was, that by
merely being among swans I had become one.*

Jacqueline Reeve

Lucy Cavendish College, 1994
Medical Sciences
Mature undergraduate, mother and farmer

It was an uphill struggle. But in my third year I just took off and had a whirl of a time – it couldn't have been better. When I got a First everyone at Lucy was thrilled for me – it's a very non-competitive college. Of course, to do this kind of thing as a women with young children (when I started mine were all under six) you do have to have a support network in the background – you need the money to buy back-up or you have to rely on your family as I did. But when I look at what I can do compared to the last generation, I realise how lucky I am. The thing is not to become too complacent. I feel I am very much an ordinary person, but I have gone out there and done it.

Clare Sambrook

Jesus College, 1982
English, Social and Political Science
Journalist

I'd never seen boys naked by moonlight, pegged to the croquet lawn. Where I came from there were no such japes, no croquet, no girls in Laura Ashley, no dining clubs. Cambridge was a shock to me and the few other working class students I met. It was my salvation too. People who at first scared me dumb became my lasting friends. I travelled to Africa thanks to College awards. I learned intellectual rigour, tasted privilege, began to see how it worked. It was a good grounding for an investigative journalist.

Wendy Savage FRCOG

Girton College, 1953
Medical Sciences
Gynaecologist and obstetrician

According to family tradition, my great-great-grandfather ran a billiard saloon in Cambridge. I was the first person in my family to go to university, and that distant connection may be one of the reasons I chose Cambridge. In the 1950s, there was a quota system which meant that only 10 per cent of medical places were for women. I would have been number 21 out of 200, so I was told I would have to wait a year. It was irritating at the time, but, in retrospect, I suppose having a fourth year, in which I had time to open my mind to history of art and psychology, was quite a good thing. I don't remember being taught by many women, but there was no overt sexism from the male lecturers. As long as the teaching was good, it didn't matter to me whether someone was male or female.

Julia Shelton

Robinson College, 1982
Engineering
Lecturer, Department of Engineering, and staff member of the IRC in
Biomedical Materials, Queen Mary and Westfield College, University
of London.

I didn't want to sit the entrance exam to Cambridge and Robinson was one of the few Colleges at the time that admitted only on interviews and A-levels. I went there in the third year that College had a full undergraduate intake, so it was exciting to be in the newest College. It was rare to be a woman doing engineering then. I remember the vast lecture halls with around 250 undergraduates and nearly all of them men. I got interested in bioengineering in my final year project. Sport, however, was my main interest, and I got a Blue for lacrosse. I have vivid memories of going up to Ryder and Amies, the sportswear shop, at the end of each week to see if I had been picked for the team. Friends are the most important thing I took away from Cambridge.

Professor Sarah Springman OBE CEng MICE

Girton College, 1975, St Catharine's College and Magdalene College (PhD)
Electrical Engineering
Professor of Geotechnical Engineering at the Swiss Federal Institute of
Technology, Zurich; international sportswoman and sporting politician

*For me, Cambridge is all about excellence – as judged externally and viewed
internally. Over the former we have little control other than to do our best
at all times. For the latter, excelling on a personal level may be equated also
with achieving one's potential – in whatever area or wherever that may be.
For many, our Cambridge experience is both a springboard to the next level
and a yardstick by which we judge the rest of our life.*

Alice Stewart MD FRCP

Girton College, 1925
Natural Sciences
Medical doctor, presenter on television's *Our Brilliant Careers*

It was the most enjoyable period of my life.

Claire Tomalin

Newnham College, 1951
English
Writer and journalist, former literary editor of the *New Statesman* and the *Sunday Times*

Three things about Cambridge that stay in my mind are, first, the happiness of being licensed to do what I anyway liked doing best: reading, and preferably lost in one of the big leather chairs in the University Library. Then the Newnham gardens, a near thing to paradise, for walking, talking, flirting, and reading in the grass on those rare days when the sun gilded them; this is a second good memory. The third is of course all the friendships made with the callow energy of youth: how amazing to find they are lasting a lifetime.

Susan Tomes

King's College, 1972
Music
Pianist

My lasting memory of Cambridge is the sensation of being surrounded by stimulating, learned people involved in all sorts of different subjects. One had only to sit in the bar for an hour to hear about literature, medicine, music, languages, and mediaeval history; it was a uniquely rich and concentrated environment. It was fascinating, too, because everyone spoke constantly about their inner lives, their hopes and fears, their struggles with identity; I didn't realise then that in later life these preoccupations would be much less openly shared. I loved the feeling of being in a hive of objective and subjective enquiry, and this remains a kind of ideal for me.

Carol Vorderman

Sidney Sussex College, 1978
Engineering
Engineer and TV presenter

*Not having had the great privilege of a classic and expensive British
education, I regard my three years in Cambridge as my finest ever
achievement. The thrill of receiving my acceptance letter has never
diminished. Cambridge is an inspiration, in one moment you feel that you
could explode with pride and the next moment you feel completely humble,
left in awe of the great minds and influences whose spirits cling heavily to
the ivory towers.*

Julia Hedgecoe

Julia Hedgecoe is one of the most noted photographers in East Anglia. Her work spans a wide range of subjects, with portraiture always a strong element. A graduate of the Guildford School of Photography, she was employed first by *The Observer*, soon moving to the freelance world and working regularly for the *The Daily Telegraph* as well as other magazines and newspapers.

Julia moved to Cambridge nine years ago. Her beautiful photographs of patchwork quilts were published in *The Patchworks of Lucy Boston* (Colt Books 1995). Five years' work photographing the high, medieval stone-carvings in Norwich Cathedral's vaulted ceilings culminated in her recent, highly-acclaimed book with medieval historian Martial Rose, *Stories in Stone* (A&C Black 1997).

In 1996 Julia completed a commission for Churchill College photographing all the College's Senior Fellows; she has worked for The Fitzwilliam Museum, *CAM* (Cambridge Alumni Magazine) and produced the photographs for *Future Solutions: The Centre for Mathematical Sciences*, a University of Cambridge fund-raising brochure. It won first place in the national Higher Education Information Services Trust Awards competition in 1997.

All Julia's photography – landscape, still life and portraiture – strongly reflects her gentle, intuitive perception.

Acknowledgments

Our first thanks must go to the portrait subjects themselves, for finding time in their very busy schedules to participate in this project. Their stories of Cambridge and their achievements after leaving here have been an inspiration to all of us.

The exhibition organisers would also like to thank the Cambridge Arts Theatre for providing an outstanding venue for the event, and particularly Nicola Upson for all of her support in making the exhibition a success.

The exhibition was made possible through support from McKinsey & Company, Barclays Bank plc, Cambridge University Press and the following Cambridge Colleges:

Churchill College, Clare College, Clare Hall, Corpus Christi College, Darwin College, Downing College, Emmanuel College, Fitzwilliam College, Girton College, Gonville and Caius College, Jesus College, King's College, Magdalene College, New Hall, Newnham College, Peterhouse, Queens' College, Robinson College, St John's College, Selwyn College, Sidney Sussex College, Trinity College, Trinity Hall, Wolfson College.

Photographic supplies were provided with a generous discount from Ilford Imaging UK Limited.

Special thanks to Louise Simpson for the initial proposal and early development of the *Educating Eve* project.

Suzi Elsden provided invaluable general assistance. Special thanks to Peter Richards for giving permission for excerpts from *CAM* (Cambridge Alumni Magazine) to be reproduced in this catalogue.

Credits

Educating Eve Working Group: Mary Broers, Juliet Campbell and Nancy Lane

Project Co-ordinator: Carol Barker

Design: Mark Mniszko

Quotes and biographical information compiled by: Pamela Davis

Photographic printing: Roy Snell

Produced by: Press and Publications Office, Vice-Chancellor's Office

Printed by: University Printing Services, University Press, Cambridge

All titles and career details given were current at the time the portraits were taken. The dates given after each subject's College are matriculation dates.

Cover photograph of Alison Duke

This exhibition catalogue has been sponsored by McKinsey & Company.

McKinsey & Company is a leading international management consultancy. We serve many of the world's most prominent organisations including multinationals, governments, charities and entrepreneurial companies. Our work cuts across all business sectors – from banking to retail, multimedia to energy, electronics to healthcare. We work with our clients on issues of importance to senior management, advising on strategy, organisation and operational issues.

As an organisation we share a strong set of values. We are a meritocracy built upon our ability to bring together the best and most distinctive people from disciplines as varied as classics and engineering. We pride ourselves on providing challenging opportunities and flexible career paths to enable our consultants to pursue their interests.

So why have we chosen to sponsor this event? In short, we, like Cambridge University, aspire to bring together the most talented and distinctive people – whatever their backgrounds. In particular, we are committed to attracting more high calibre women into business and consulting. This exhibition highlights the enormous achievements of female alumnae in all walks of life. We are proud and privileged to be associated with such a celebration of talent.